# Silver and Bold | On Financial Planning

Living a Fearless Life Post-55

Lee Hathaway

Three Triangles Publishing

# Contents

# Introduction

For many, retirement is the light at the end of the tunnel, the pot of gold after decades of hard work. It's a time to relax, pursue passions, and enjoy simple pleasures.

But retirement can also seem daunting. After 30 or 40 years at a job, how do you adapt to a completely open schedule? Will you have the savings to maintain your lifestyle for potentially 20+ years? What will give your days meaning and structure?

This book aims to help illuminate the path, providing knowledge to equip you for this monumental life transition.

Within these pages, we'll explore the key areas you must address as retirement approaches - from practical financial matters to lifestyle and personal decisions. This multi-faceted look will help you build a retirement plan tailored to your unique dreams and aspirations.

We'll begin by discussing the foundation - your financial plan. Establishing your retirement budget, assessing income sources, and creating intelligent investment strategies are fundamental building blocks. You'll get tips to help grow your nest egg, maximize returns, and ensure your savings can successfully fund your retirement time-frame.

Taxes take a significant bite out of retirement income. We'll explore ways to minimize your tax liability and get strategic with drawing down retirement accounts. You'll also learn how to reduce the tax impact on your estate to pass on more wealth to your beneficiaries.

Housing is another primary consideration. Weighing options like downsizing, relocating, or home modifications for aging in place are vital decisions. You'll get guidance on the pros and cons of each to make the choice that best supports your lifestyle.

Of course, health becomes a priority as you age. We'll provide suggestions to supplement Medicare, estimate future health costs, and ensure you have necessary care directives. Protecting your health and wealth go hand-in-hand.

Retirement also presents an opportunity to rediscover old passions and uncover new ones. You'll get ideas for hobbies, volunteering, travel, and more to keep you active and engaged. We'll also share tips for strengthening social connections and community bonds, which are vital for mental health.

While in-depth financial knowledge would require several volumes, this book aims to distill the crucial basics - budgeting, claiming Social Security, investing, managing taxes, and healthcare costs. With clear examples and actionable tips, you'll learn approaches to help secure your financial future.

However, as mentioned, retirement is about more than just money. We also address essential lifestyle elements - your interests, relationships, ideal living arrangements, and finding purpose. These facets help shape the day-to-day experience of retirement.

Keep in mind that there is no one-size-fits-all plan. Retirement is a profoundly personal journey. Your dreams, passions, and needs all influence the choices you make.

Throughout the book, we suggest strategies and encourage self-reflection to tailor your custom-made plans. Do you envision a peaceful country retreat or cultural immersion in a foreign land? Is a second career on your horizon? The path you forge will be unique.

Yes, the thought of such a sweeping change can seem daunting initially. But that's why we're here - to be your guide. These pages aim to make a complex topic understandable. To break retirement planning down into achievable steps. To spark ideas for living your retirement to the fullest.

The door to this next chapter of life is opening. Let's walk through it together - equipped, informed, and ready to embrace the possibilities ahead. Your dreams await.

# Section 1: Retirement Goals

Retirement presents endless possibilities, but first, you must define your destination before mapping out the journey. This opening section will help spark ideas and provide guidance on crafting retirement goals that align with your passions, interests, and aspirations. You'll get tips on building your ideal vision and devising plans to make that vision a reality. With your goals clarified, you can make more informed choices when navigating the practical aspects of retirement planning.

# Chapter One

## Achieving the Lifestyle You Want in Retirement

### Visualizing Your Unique Retirement Lifestyle

Discovering your 'retired self' goes beyond assuming a one-size-fits-all lifestyle that comes with growing older. Retirees today are breaking stereotypes and living diverse, dynamic lives. Your retirement should reflect who you are, peppered with freedom you haven't had since before you started working full-time.

Before you crack the numbers and devise investment strategies, start with the heart of it all - your retirement vision.

- Think about what brings you joy: Is it that cottage near the beach you've always dreamed of? Or is it the thrill of wandering in new cities?

- Maybe it's the chance to delve back into hobbies and passions that fell by the wayside during your career. Are there unfinished novels you want to write or a garden you want to cultivate?

- Remember your social needs. Do you crave the bustle of family and friends or the serenity of solitude and nature?

- Picture your everyday. What does a regular Tuesday look like for you?

Pause for a moment and visualize it. Imagine yourself living that life. What does it feel like? Are there multiple scenarios you're equally drawn to? If yes, consider that flexibility might be a crucial component of your retirement life.

An exercise such as this requires introspection and honesty. It's not about the 'shoulds' but what you truly desire. Don't limit yourself or cut corners - this is your space to dream.

Once you have a clear picture, or pictures, of what your ideal retirement looks like, you are better equipped for the next planning stage. These vision(s) will act as a guiding star, helping you make informed and relevant decisions toward achieving your unique retirement lifestyle.

Remember, retirement is not a finite state but a dynamic phase of life that can last multiple decades. Your aspirations, health, and circumstances may change, and that's okay. The key is ensuring your retirement plan is as flexible and evolving as life. Stay true to your aspirations, keep reassessing, and pivot when required. The goal isn't a perfect retirement - it's an ideal retirement for you.

## Crafting Your Retirement Plan

Now that you have vividly imagined your unique retirement lifestyle, it's time to translate that vision into tangible, practical plans. Your retirement plan isn't just a financial strategy; it's a blueprint for realizing your dream lifestyle.

Let's visualize a scenario: Meet John, a 55-year-old marketing manager who loves gardening and travel. John pictures spending his days in a small cottage, gardening, reading during his downtime, and exploring new cities once or twice a year. Now, let's see how John would craft his retirement plan:

- **Determine Your Retirement Budget:** Based on his envisioned lifestyle, John calculates his retirement budget. He considers the cost of a small cottage, gardening tools, traveling expenses, and everyday living costs. Your retirement budget should be based on your current expenses and aligned with your aspirations for your post-retirement life.

- **Plan For Health-Related Costs:** John is relatively healthy now but knows that health complications may arise as he ages. He includes potential medical costs as part of his retirement budget, ensuring he has a contingency plan to avoid any financial stress that could blur his dream lifestyle.

- **Factor in Long-term Care:** John also considers that there might come a time when he might need assistance with everyday activities. Determining the potential need for long-term care is wise when crafting your retirement plan.

Developing a plan might seem daunting. However, remember that retirement planning is not solely a financial process; it's about devising a strategy that allows you to pursue your passions and live your dream lifestyle in retirement. This vision will motivate you to stick to your plan and make the process more meaningful and enjoyable.

The specifics of your plan will depend on your unique vision of retirement. A good plan considers your financial resources and aligns with your aspirations, preparing you for your exciting next chapter.

## Creating Investment Strategies Centered on Your Retirement Vision

After crafting your plan, the trick lies in funding it—this is where an investment strategy becomes essential. However, it's crucial to remember that our investment approach should align with our retirement vision and mirror our risk tolerance, time horizon, and financial goals.

- **Diversify Your Portfolio:** A diversified portfolio helps to manage risk while allowing room for growth. From our previous scenario, John would need to balance his investments between high-risk, high-return avenues that could fund his travel and low-risk options for his day-to-day expenses.

- **Maintain a Long-term "Future-focused" Perspective:** Remember, retirement investment is a marathon, not a sprint. Maintain a forward-looking mindset, as John would, considering his everyday needs and long-term goals like maintaining his cottage and funding his travels.

- **Adopt a Disciplined Investment Approach:** Stay consistent with your investments. For John, regular additions to his portfolio, regardless of market highs and lows, could result in significant potential savings, ensuring his gardening and travel dreams don't wilt.

- **Keep Tabs on Your Investments:** Regularly review your portfolio to ensure it aligns with your retirement goals. As John nears retirement, he may want to reassess his strategy, shifting towards more conservative investments to help secure what he's accumulated.

Remember, the right investment strategy depends on your retirement vision. It's essential to align your financial decisions with your lifestyle expectations in retirement so your monetary resources support your golden years' dreams. The objective isn't just financial security, life satisfaction, and fulfillment in retirement.

## Incorporating Health and Well-being Into Your Retirement Vision

A significant component of your retirement lifestyle is maintaining your health. Creating a physical, mental, and emotional well-being plan is as crucial as crafting your financial plan. After all, you must be healthy to enjoy a picturesque cottage or adventurous travels.

In John's case, he enjoys gardening, which fulfills his passion and provides a form of physical activity. Let's have a look at how John incorporates health and well-being into his retirement plans:

- **Engaging in Regular Exercise:** Gardening is John's choice of staying active. He also plans to take regular beach walks near his dreamed-of cottage. Staying active would be critical to his physical health and independence as he ages.

- **Eating a Balanced Diet:** As someone who loves to garden, John plans to grow some of his food, incorporating fresh vegetables and fruits into his diet. He's aware that good nutrition is crucial for his health, longevity, and overall quality of life.

- **Prioritizing Mental Wellness:** John loves reading, which will keep his mind sharp. Traveling to new cities and learning about different cultures will stimulate his mind and keep life exciting.

- **Regular Health Check-ups:** John plans to have regular medical checkups and health evaluations to catch any potential issues early. He's calculated the possible cost of these medical visits into his retirement plan.

- **Planning for Long-term Care:** John realizes he may need assistance as he ages. He's considered long-term care costs and included them in his plan.

Remember, the goal is to plan for a life that brings you joy and fulfillment in your golden years, and good health is the underpinning to live that life to the fullest. As such, incorporating a strategy for maintaining health should not be an afterthought but a central part of your retirement planning.

Retirement presents a unique opportunity in life, a chance to reclaim your time and live it precisely how you desire. But to do so requires a shift in perspective. Rather than viewing retirement as a singular financial goal, consider it a tapestry that weaves your lifestyle aspirations, financial planning, health, and well-being together.

Remember, John's story is just an example. Your ideal retirement could look entirely different. You may envision a life filled with new academic pursuits, philanthropic endeavors, or close-knit family times. The key is to ensure that each aspect – your lifestyle vision, financial strategies, and health considerations – aligns uniquely with you.

The planning might seem daunting now, but remember, it's not just about building a nest egg. It's about creating a blueprint for your future – a future where every day is a manifestation of your passions, interests, and aspirations.

So, take a moment. Visualize. Plan. Dream. Because a well-planned retirement isn't just about surviving. It's about thriving in a life that's tailor-made for you.

# Chapter Two

## Planning to Retire in Another Country

Retirement can be the perfect time to change your lifestyle and location. Maybe you've always dreamed of living on a sun-soaked Mediterranean island or being absorbed in the vibrant culture of a Southeast Asian country. This section will provide an overview of essential factors when considering retiring in another country.

### Research The Destination

### Cost of Living

Unlike the transient costs you experience on vacation, choosing to retire in a new country comes with a more complex financial picture. The web of groceries, utilities, property expenses, taxes, healthcare, and entertainment weaves a different tapestry in each corner of the world. And this tapestry, your new cost of living, can gently caress or significantly eat into your retirement nest egg.

- Analyzing Essential Commodities and Services: To paint an

accurate financial picture of your retirement abroad, reach out to local grocery stores or markets to get an idea of everyday food prices. Compare utility costs and services between your current and potential destination. And don't forget the luxuries that bring joy to your retirement; how much does a round of golf, a dinner out, or a theater ticket cost?

- Grasping the Tax Scheme: Tax can be an invisible hand digging into your pocket if you're not careful. Connect with a local tax expert and explore websites like the Organization for Economic Co-operation and Development (OECD) to grasp how the local tax scheme may apply to you.

- Investigating Real Estate: Whether you plan to buy or rent, knowing your potential housing costs is vital. A city-center apartment in Paris will cost you vastly different from a countryside home in Costa Rica. Network with local real estate agents to understand the market or use online platforms to compare rental and purchasing prices across your shortlisted destinations.

While destinations with a lower cost of living may seem attractive, weigh these against other factors like healthcare, safety, and lifestyle preferences to find the sweet spot for your retirement adventure.

## Local Laws and Regulations

Every country dancing to its rhythm of legal intricacies forms a vital part of your retirement planning. These range from how you become a resident to how you buy properties and pay your taxes - each displaying marked differences across borders.

- Grasping the Visa Quandaries: Each country has unique visa requirements and processes. For instance, some countries offer special retirement visas, like Malaysia's "Malaysia My Second Home" (MM2H) program. Research and understand your potential destination's visa process to avoid unpleasant surprises.

- Navigating Property Ownership: Laws about foreign property ownership vary widely. Some countries welcome it, some restrict it, and others complicate it. In Mexico, for instance, foreigners cannot outright own land within 50 kilometers of the coast or 100 kilometers of international borders, but they can hold it in a trust. Get a grasp of these regulations before making any decisions.

- Understanding Taxes: Local and national taxes can severely dent your retirement budget if not planned correctly. Countries like Portugal offer a Non-Habitual Residence (NHR) scheme that can result in significant tax benefits for retirees.

Being unaware of or misunderstanding these laws and regulations can lead to complications down the line, so invest your time in understanding them well. Consider seeking professional guidance to ensure you know all the necessary details before moving.

## Health Care

Healthcare is a critical factor to consider before making your move. Healthcare systems vary broadly from country to country - from free at the point of delivery systems, insurance-based models, to out-of-pocket models with little government involvement.

- Exploring Public and Private Health Coverage: Find out whether the nation's public healthcare system is accessible to retirees from abroad, the types of services covered, and the potential treatment wait times. Private healthcare can offer more comfort and shorter waiting times, but it comes at a higher cost. Weigh both options against your budget and healthcare needs.

- Discovering Overseas Health Insurance Plans: Look into international health insurance plans that cover treatment in various countries. Factors include coverage limit, the network of healthcare providers, and whether a pre-existing condition is covered.

- Understanding Health Infrastructure: Research the state of healthcare infrastructure - hospitals, clinics, and healthcare professionals - in your potential retirement destination. Factor in the speed of emergency services and the availability of specialized treatments.

Given healthcare's high cost and importance, you must dedicate substantial time to researching and understanding your chosen country's healthcare system.

## Language and Culture

Immersing yourself in a new culture and language can be a thrilling adventure, but it also presents challenges and opportunities. As you transition to your retirement destination, understanding the country's culture and language is more than just essential; it's transformative.

- Mastering the Language Basics: Engage in language learning before your move. This will facilitate smoother interactions and offer rich insights into the country's way of life. You are brushing up on essential phrases or taking language classes for a few months before your move can make a difference.

- Embracing the Local Customs, Traditions, and Lifestyle: Understanding local customs and traditions is vital to appreciate and truly become a part of your new community. Research, ask questions, and remain open-minded to unfamiliar practices. For instance, removing your shoes before entering a home is customary in Japan. Personal space may be much closer in Spain than you're accustomed to.

Remember, entering a new culture is like reading a book for the first time - understanding the narrative takes time and patience, but the resulting richness of experience is deeply rewarding.

## Making The Move

After thoroughly researching and satisfying yourself with the potential destination, it's time to begin moving. This transition involves more than just practical planning; it also includes preparing yourself emotionally for the changes ahead:

- Plan and Organize Your Finances: Now that you've surveyed your destination's cost of living, including tax implications and healthcare costs, incorporate these into a comprehensive financial plan. This will help ease your transition and allow you to enjoy your retirement with peace of mind.

- Consider Downsizing And Managing Your Properties At

Home: Consider what you'll do with your current abode – sell, rent, or leave it under someone's care. Each option comes with its considerations and consequences. You'll also need to think about what to do with your belongings. A new space means a new lifestyle, which may require a downsized and curated selection of your possessions.

- Think About How to Stay Connected With Your Family And Friends Back Home: Leaving your home country doesn't mean cutting ties with your dear ones. Evaluate your communication options - from regular phone calls and video chats to social media interactions. Plan regular visits if possible. This emotional support system will be valuable as you adjust to your new life.

Making the move to retire in a different country can be an enriching and exciting phase of life, but it also requires thorough planning and preparation. Addressing both practical and emotional aspects can facilitate a smoother transition from a regular resident to a global retiree. Remember that planning for your dream retirement destination is never too early. Here's to your new adventure!

Embarking on retirement in a different country can be an invigorating journey - a new chapter teeming with discovery and excitement. However, this adventure also demands meticulous planning, comprehensive research, and thoughtful preparation. By diving deep into the nuances of the cost of living, local laws and regulations, healthcare systems, and cultural landscapes, you're equipping yourself with information and confidence to navigate this new path. Moreover, remember to plan for the emotional aspects of the move, maintain connections with your loved ones, and embrace the transformative journey ahead of you. In doing so, the transition from being a regular resident to becoming an enriched global retiree will be smoother and more fulfilling. Start early, weigh your options wisely, and let the countdown to your dream retirement destination begin. Here's to diving into your exciting new chapter, and happy travels!

# Chapter Three

---

# Planning For Long-Term Care Amid Retirement

Dealing with the prospects of retirement can be a daunting journey, one that is filled with lots of questions and uncertainties. One pressing issue we often grapple with is the certainty of long-term care.

## Understanding Long-Term Care And Its Necessity

An essential step to preparing for long-term care is understanding what it is. Long-term care includes a wide range of medical and support services for people with a degenerative condition, a prolonged illness, or a disability. It ranges from assistance with routine daily activities like eating, bathing, or dressing to skilled care provided by nurses, therapists, or other professionals.

## How to Plan for Long-Term Care

Planning for this phase of life as early as possible is crucial to help reduce stress and anxiety. Here are some considerations:

- **Evaluate Your Health Risks:** Understanding your health

risks and family history will help you estimate the care you or your loved one might require. It also helps to visualize the type of long-term care facility or setup you might be most comfortable with.

- **Understand Your Financial Resources:** A thorough review of your assets, retirement benefits, pensions, and other monetary savings can help you build a financial plan to afford long-term care if needed.

- **Consider Long-Term Care Insurance:** This is designed to cover long-term services and support. It helps cover the cost of care not covered by health insurance, Medicare, or Medicaid.

- **Plan for Home Care Services:** Depending on the level of care needed, you might want to look into home care services. This allows you to live at home while still receiving the necessary help.

## From Planning to Action: Enacting Your Long-Term Care Strategy

After gathering the necessary information and considering your care options, the next step is implementing these plans. Moving from contemplation to action can sometimes feel abrupt, but it's a crucial phase in securing your future care.

Start by opening up a dialogue with your family members. Discuss your long-term care preferences, potential options, and any concerns you or they may have. Remember, these conversations might not be easy, but they are essential in ensuring everyone is on the same page.

In addition to these conversations, consider taking some tangible steps toward your long-term care. This could be as simple as modifying your house to make it safer and more accessible or as involved as researching and visiting potential retirement communities or nursing homes.

Long-term care planning can be overwhelming, but remember, the earlier you begin this journey, the more prepared you will be. A concrete plan offers peace of mind and ensures that you and your loved ones have access to the care they may need. You can look forward to a secure and more enjoyable retirement by taking action today, knowing you have prepared for potential challenges.

# Chapter Four

## Planning For Retirement: Allocating Time Wisely

R etirement can be a time of profound change, freedom, and transformation. You are given back many hours daily, and planning how to use this time effectively and enjoyably is essential. Below, we'll explore how to allocate time during retirement and consider taking up new hobbies and activities.

### Deciding On Time Allocation

- **Unearth your hidden interests and passions**. Retirement is an opportunity to dive into the depths of your desires. Have you always wanted to study the stars, brew beer, or learn to play an instrument? Now is the time to bring these latent passions to the forefront of your planning.

- **Infuse creativity into physical activities**. While incorporating a routine of physical activities is essential, make it unique. Instead of just a daily walk, how about bird-watching treks, dance lessons, or Tai Chi in the park? Choose activities that blend health and personal interest.

- **Allocate time for unconventional learning**. Retirement is your personal Renaissance. Go beyond just learning new crafts, skills, or languages. How about studying archeology, learning magic tricks, or even coding? Ignite your intellectual spirit with something out of the ordinary.

- **Adopt a radical approach to giving back.** Volunteering can be more than teaching kids or helping at local community centers. What about using your professional skills to consult for non-profits, build homes with a local charity, or get involved in citizen science projects? Challenge the traditional concepts of volunteer work.

Remember, retirement is your canvas, and you are the artist. Paint it with vibrant colors of curiosity, health, learning, and altruism.

## Taking Up New Hobbies And Activities

Choosing new hobbies and activities to pursue is an exciting part of planning for retirement. Here are a few suggestions:

- **Drone Flying.** This modern hobby provides fun and opens a world of photography and exploration possibilities. Imagine capturing beautiful aerial shots of your city or a stunning sunset over a forest!

- **Local Theater Group.** Participating in a local theater group can offer a creative outlet and a strong sense of community, whether acting, set design, or production.

- **Cheese Making.** Creating your cheese can be a rewarding process. Plus, it's a great talking point when serving hand-made delicacies to friends and family.

- **Digital Art.** With numerous online resources, learning to create digital art has never been more accessible. From 3D modeling to digital painting, this can be a fun and modern take on the conventional arts and crafts retirement activity.

- **Culinary Exploration.** Retirement is the perfect time to delve into the world of gastronomy. Try exotic recipes, learn about wine pairing, or start a food blog to share your cooking adventures.

Remember, these are just prompts. The beauty of retirement is the freedom to follow your path and discover new passions and interests.

## Navigating The Challenges of Retirement

While retirement opens up a world of possibilities, it's also important to acknowledge the potential hurdles and prepare for them.

- **Age-Related Limitations**. As we age, we may need to adjust our expectations and activities. For example, that dream of climbing Mount Everest might be better fulfilled through an immersive virtual reality experience or a helicopter tour. There's always a way to adapt your interests and passions to suit your capabilities.

- **Financial Constraints**. While you might be free of work-related responsibilities, financial limitations can still affect your retirement. It's essential to budget for your new hobbies and interests. Remember, many fulfilling activities don't require significant financial investments. Local libraries, community centers, and online resources can be treasure troves of low-cost or free experiences.

- **Lack of Social Support**. Retirement can sometimes feel isolating, mainly if you're used to a bustling work environment. However, there are numerous ways to stay socially connected. Join clubs or groups that share your interests, volunteer in your community, or even start your meet-up group. Technology can also be a powerful tool for staying connected with friends and family, near and far.

Every challenge you face during retirement can be turned into an opportunity with some creativity and planning. Be adaptable, be resourceful, and above all, be open to new experiences. This is your time to shine.

Retirement is not the end; it's the beginning of new adventures. It's all about planning how best to use your time to pivot toward a satisfying, fulfilling retirement period filled with learning, exploration, and new experiences. Stay active, keep learning, and don't forget to dedicate some time to give back to the community. Remember to be adaptable in the face of age-related limitations, be resourceful to overcome financial constraints, and harness the power of technology to maintain social connections. Time is what you make of it now, more so than ever. Make it count.

# Section 2 - Financial Considerations

While retirement opens up free time, you still need the financial resources to fund your desired lifestyle. This section explores vital monetary considerations like budgeting, managing investments, estimates for savings, and strategies for generating retirement income. You'll learn ways to grow your nest egg, maximize Social Security benefits, minimize taxes, and calculate projected costs - equipping you with the knowledge to make intelligent financial decisions.

# Chapter Five

## How Much Income Will You Need Annually Post-Retirement?

R etirement isn't just about winding down; for many, it's a new beginning, a chance to live dreams deferred due to work commitments. Whether you envision a second career, philanthropy activities, or becoming a globe-trotter, the question remains: How much income will you need annually to make these dreams come true post-retirement? Determining this isn't as simple as following generic advice -- it's a profoundly personal calculation tailored to your unique aspirations. So, let's consider and debunk the one-size-fits-all myth and create a retirement plan that's as unique as you are.

### Identifying Your Needs

Planning for retirement is not a one-size-fits-all journey. Everyone has unique needs and lifestyle choices that will shape their golden years. Here's how to make an estimation that genuinely reflects your circumstances.

## Estimating Annual Spending

Your spending habits during retirement will depend on the kind of life you envision post-retirement. While some might see it as a chance to travel the world, others might find joy in the simple pleasures of home or take up hobbies that had been pushed to the back burner due to work commitments.

- Begin by crafting a "mock" retirement budget. Instead of the standard rule of thumb to estimate your annual spending in retirement as 70% to 80% of your pre-retirement income, build a detailed budget that includes everything from groceries to travel plans. This will give you a more realistic estimate of your annual expenses.

- Consider the potential changes in your lifestyle. Perhaps you plan on downsizing your home or relocating to a city with a lower cost of living. Incorporate these changes into your budget.

- Don't overlook the impact of inflation. It's not enough to plan for expenses in today's terms. Consider how inflation will decrease your purchasing power in the future and adjust your budget accordingly.

## Unexpected Expenses

Life can throw curveballs, and it's essential to have a plan for unexpected expenses.

- Factor in healthcare costs: As we age, medical expenses can become a significant part of our budget. While Medicare will cover some costs, many expenses will come out-of-pocket. Remember to account for long-term care facilities, home care, and other health-related costs that can add up.

- Build an emergency fund: A robust emergency fund can distinguish between a stress-free retirement and one filled with financial worries. Aim to save enough to cover at least six months of living expenses.

- Prepare for home and car repairs: If you own a home or car, they'll inevitably need repairs or maintenance. Include these potential costs in your retirement plan.

By tailoring your retirement planning to your unique needs and circumstances, you'll be better prepared to enjoy your golden years without financial stress. Remember, it's not just about surviving retirement but truly living it.

## Setting Up Your Retirement Plan

Creating a robust retirement plan involves more than simply saving a portion of your income. It requires strategic planning and a deep understanding of your financial toolkit. Here's how to maximize your retirement income while keeping risk manageable.

### Investment Returns

Your investment returns will play a pivotal role in determining your annual income during retirement.

- Estimate conservatively: Err on the side of caution when predicting your returns. It's safer to assume a modest return and be pleasantly surprised than to count on achieving lofty stock market returns every year.

- Diversify intelligently: Diversification is more than owning a mix of stocks and bonds. Consider alternative investment opportunities like real estate, peer-to-peer lending, or investing in a small business. These can provide substantial returns and further diversify your income stream.

- Regular adjustments: Keep an eye on your portfolio and make adjustments regularly. This isn't just about rebalancing and reconsidering your risk tolerance as you approach retirement.

## Social Security

Social Security is a safety net for many retirees, but there's more to this system than meets the eye.

- Calculate your expected payout using the Social Security Administration tool. But remember, that's only part of the picture.

- Time your benefits carefully. You can begin claiming Social Security at 62, but waiting until you're older can significantly increase your monthly payout. Consider the trade-offs: Will the immediate income benefit you more now, or is it worth waiting for more extensive checks later?

- Understand the taxation of Social Security benefits. Many people don't realize that depending on your income, a portion of your benefits may be taxable. Make sure to factor this into your planning.

Retirement planning can be complex and may require professional advice. It's also a moving target, as factors like inflation, market conditions, and spending habits can change over time. However, estimating your income needs accurately and planning wisely will improve your chances of a comfortable, stress-free retirement. Always be proactive, plan for changes, and be in a solid position to truly enjoy your golden years.

# Chapter Six

---

# How Much Should You Have In Your Retirement Accounts?

F inancial security in retirement doesn't just happen. It takes planning, commitment, and, most importantly, money. Unpacking your retirement savings can be daunting, but we're here to help answer one fundamental question if you're one of the individuals preparing for retirement: How much savings do you currently have in your retirement accounts?

## Avoiding the Fear of Lifelong Savings

Many of us falter at the thought of retirement savings due to the emotions it can stir – fear, insecurity, and feelings of inadequacy. It's natural to feel overwhelmed when faced with the idea of saving for a few decades down the line. But let's shift this perspective.

Think of it as a journey rather than a daunting task. Start by acknowledging where you currently stand with your savings. This isn't an exercise to induce guilt but to establish a starting point.

Next, strive to create a healthy relationship with your savings. Every dollar saved is a step towards financial security, not a sacrifice of present joys. Remember, you're planning for a comfortable future without constantly worrying about finances.

Finally, educating yourself can significantly reduce the fear associated with retirement savings. Understanding different investment options, learning about compound interest, and realizing the benefits of starting early can make the process far less intimidating. Over time, this knowledge can make saving and investing a rewarding part of your life.

Put fear aside and welcome financial literacy and confidence on this journey to a secure retirement.

## The Reality of Retirement Savings

Let's now tackle the tangible part of retirement savings - the numbers. According to a recent study conducted by Fidelity Investments, the average 50-year-old should have approximately six times their annual salary saved for retirement.

- If your annual salary is $80,000, you should aim to have around $480,000 in your retirement accounts.

- A good target for those earning $100,000 annually would be to have about $600,000 stashed away.

But remember, these are just guidelines. We all have individual circumstances, lifestyles, and retirement dreams that can affect how much we should truly aim to save. It doesn't mean you've failed if you don't have these exact amounts in your accounts.

Moreover, these figures are not intended to scare you but to provide a realistic benchmark. It's all about setting achievable goals and committing to a plan to reach them. You might be surprised at how quickly your savings can grow with regular contributions and intelligent investment strategies.

Next, we'll look at some tips for building your retirement savings.

## Suggestions for Building Your Retirement Savings

Do these numbers seem overwhelming? They don't have to be. Here are some strategies for building your retirement nest egg:

- Regular contributions: Make sure you contribute as much as possible to your retirement savings. Small amounts over time can accumulate significantly due to the compound interest.

- Diversifying your Investments: Diversifying your portfolio can help you balance risk and return. Talk to a financial advisor about the best investment strategies for your needs.

- Taking advantage of tax benefits: Retirement savings accounts like IRAs and 401(k)s come with tax benefits. These accounts can significantly boost your savings by reducing your tax liability.

Retirement savings are personal and different for everyone, based on income, lifestyle, and plans. However, it's important to remember that it's never too late to begin or to bolster your retirement savings.

Preparing for retirement should not involve anxiety or fear; from a realistic standpoint, even commencing or catching up on savings in your 50s can provide you with a comfortable retirement cushion. Instead, allow these numbers to motivate you professionally and personally to plan better, to hustle more dedicatedly, and to encourage ongoing saving patterns.

There's no time like the present. Picture your retirement dreams and start planning today! It's your future — make it a financially secure one.

# Chapter Seven

# How Will Inflation Affect Your Retirement Savings?

As you blow out the candles on your 50th birthday cake, retirement might seem like a well-earned, tranquil shore in the not-so-distant future. But before you set sail, there's a storm you need to weather—its name is inflation. It's an economic phenomenon that can silently erode the value of your retirement savings, transforming your calm retirement plan into a storm of financial concern. So, let's tackle the question that should be at the helm of your retirement planning: "How exactly does inflation impact your retirement savings, and what can you do about it?"

## Understanding the Basics

Before we dive deeper, let's simplify the concept of inflation. Think of inflation as a game of musical chairs. You're circling a set of goods and services (the chairs) with your money (the players). When the music (economic activity) runs smoothly, there are enough chairs for everyone. But when inflation (the game's speed) picks up, it's like removing chairs from the game. Suddenly, your money must scramble harder to claim the same goods or services.

To put it in concrete terms, suppose you have $100 today. If the annual inflation rate is 2%, you will need $102 to buy the same basket of items next year. That's inflation, slyly pulling chairs and forcing your money to work harder for the same spot.

## Role of Inflation in Retirement Planning

Now, how does this concept of inflation transfer to your retirement savings?

### Rising Living Costs

To start - Day-to-day expenses inevitably rise over time due to inflation. This means your retirement savings must be significant enough to finance the increased cost of living post-retirement. Remember, you might no longer have a regular income to help keep pace with these rising costs.

### Diminished Purchasing Power

Inflation can significantly diminish an individual's cash flow purchasing power from pension plans and annuity investments.

- For example, if your retirement income is $40,000 today, and the inflation rate is at 2%, you will need an income of approximately $48,800 ten years later.

### Investment Returns

Inflation also affects your investment returns. Without the right strategy, your savings may not accumulate at the expected rate, potentially leaving you with less retirement income.

## Navigating Different Inflation Rates in Retirement Planning

Inflation isn't a constant—it fluctuates. Depending on the economic climate, we might face low, moderate, or high inflation rates. Each scenario poses a unique challenge, and your retirement planning should adapt accordingly.

### Low Inflation

Low inflation, typically around 1-2%, might seem harmless. But even this can quietly erode your savings over time. The effect is like a slow leak in a tire—hardly noticeable at first, but eventually, it'll leave you flat. Your savings and investments must grow at least at the inflation rate to keep pace.

### Moderate Inflation

In times of moderate inflation, typically around 3-4%, the costs of goods and services increase more noticeably. Your purchasing power can be quickly undermined if your income doesn't keep up. Hence, your investments should match and exceed the inflation rate to maintain your lifestyle.

### High Inflation

High inflation, anything over 5%, is a storm on the horizon. It can ravage your savings and drastically reduce your purchasing power. In such a climate, defensive strategies are crucial. Consider assets that tend to increase in value during inflationary periods, like real estate, commodities, or inflation-protected securities.

Remember: the inflation rate isn't just a number—it's a significant factor that can shape your retirement journey. Consider different inflation scenarios and strategize to protect your hard-earned nest egg as you plan.

## Planning for Inflation in Retirement

While inflation can pose significant challenges, it's not an unbeatable foe. With strategic planning and astute financial decisions, you can safeguard your retirement savings against the potential pitfalls of inflation.

- **Consider TIPS:** Treasury Inflation-Protected Securities are a type of U.S. treasury bond designed to help investors protect their investments against inflation. The principle of a TIPS increases with inflation while the interest rate remains fixed, providing a reliable safeguard during high inflation periods.

- **Investments in Stocks:** Over the long run, stocks have historically delivered returns that outpace inflation. Although they come with higher risk, investing a portion of your retirement savings in stocks could provide a buffer against inflation.

- **Look into Annuities:** Some annuities are designed to counter inflation. A step-up annuity, for example, period-

ically adjusts benefits payments to help keep up with inflation. Explore annuity options that offer inflation protection,
but be sure to weigh the costs and benefits.

- **Diversify Your Investments:** Certain assets like real estate
  and commodities can benefit during high inflation. Diversifying your portfolio to include these assets can protect your
  retirement savings from inflation's harsh impact.

Remember: Inflation can be a challenge, especially regarding
your retirement planning. However, with informed decisions and
thoughtful planning, you can sail smoothly toward retirement, regardless of economic weather. The earlier you start planning, the better placed you will be to ensure a comfortable and secure retirement.
So, as you chart your course toward your golden years, keep a keen
eye on inflation trends and their potential impact on your retirement
savings.

# Chapter Eight

## The Comfort Zone: Navigating Investments for Your Retirement

### The Psychology of Investing

Investing isn't just a financial act; it's a psychological one. Our attitudes toward money and risk-taking are deeply rooted in our upbringing, life experiences, and biology. Understanding your psychological relationship with money can illuminate your investing style, risk tolerance, and decisions. Ask yourself what emotions arise when you think about money: Excitement? Anxiety? Indifference? These feelings can be a compass guiding your investment strategy.

### Financial Security in the Modern Age

Today's economic landscape is significantly different from that of previous generations. With longer lifespans, the rising cost of healthcare, and evolving job markets, understanding what constitutes financial security has shifted. It's not just about accumulating wealth anymore; it's about sustainability, adaptability, and weathering market volatility.

## The Social Aspect of Investing

Investing is also a social phenomenon. The communities we're part of, the media we consume, and our conversations can significantly influence our investing decisions. Recognizing these influences and seeking diverse perspectives is crucial to gaining a more rounded view of the financial markets and potential opportunities.

## Beyond the Basics: Advanced Investment Concepts

Beyond knowing what stocks and bonds are, consider how different investment vehicles can serve your long-term goals. Learn about the effects of compound interest over time, the benefits of diversified portfolios, and the implications of market trends on various asset classes. Furthermore, technological innovations have given rise to robo-advisors and investment apps, democratizing access to financial markets and raising questions about human advisors' role in the digital age.

## Financial Education as a Tool

Empowering yourself with financial education is a critical step toward long-term security. Understanding basic investment principles like risk and return, inflation, and asset allocation can transform your approach to investing. However, the goal isn't just to accumulate knowledge—it's to apply that knowledge to create a robust, flexible retirement strategy that can adapt to your changing life circumstances and the dynamic financial landscape.

## Are You Comfortable With Investing?

Before jumping headfirst into the investing world, gauging your comfort level is crucial. Let's explore some common concerns:

### Fear of Risk

Investing comes with potential risks. As the value of investments can go up, they can also go down. Hence, it's important only to make informed decisions.

### Lack of Knowledge

Many individuals may feel hesitant towards investing due to unfamiliarity with financial jargon or the mechanics of the stock market. Much of this can be mitigated with education and enlisting the help of professionals.

### Managing Your Investments

Once you're comfortable investing, the next step is to devise a successful strategy for managing your investments. Here are some key considerations to incorporate into your investment plan:

### Regular Portfolio Review

Performing regular check-ins on your investments isn't just about monitoring their performance. It's a chance to reassess your financial goals and adjust your portfolio to align with them. Set a quarterly, biannually, or annual review schedule for these reviews. When reviewing, consider factors like how close you are to retirement, changes in your income, and any new financial goals.

## Diversification

Don't put all your eggs in one basket. Diversifying your investment portfolio can help mitigate risk. This involves spreading your investments across various asset classes, such as stocks, bonds, and real estate. The right mix will depend on your risk tolerance and investment horizon.

## Rebalancing

Rebalancing is the process of realigning the proportions of your portfolio to maintain your desired level of risk and return. As market performance can cause your portfolio's asset allocation to shift, it's essential to rebalance periodically.

## Seeking Professional Assistance

Investment planning can be complex. It might be beneficial to seek the help of a financial advisor. They can better understand your investment options and help you devise a strategy tailored to your unique needs and financial goals. Remember, a good advisor should be able to explain complex concepts in a way you understand.

Remember, investing is a journey, not a destination. Stay patient, keep learning, and adapt your strategy as needed. This systematic and educated approach to managing your investments can contribute to a more secure and comfortable retirement.

## Embrace Your Investment Journey

Investing isn't just about numbers on a balance sheet; it's a deeply personal journey that intertwines with our life experiences, social influences, and individual risk tolerance. By understanding these factors and educating ourselves on basic and advanced investment concepts, we empower ourselves to make informed decisions that can contribute significantly to our long-term financial security.

It's crucial to remember that investing isn't a race. It's a step-by-step process that requires regular portfolio reviews, diversification, rebalancing, and professional guidance. Each decision should align with your financial goals, risk tolerance, and comfort level with investing.

So keep learning, start small, seek help, and lean on your support systems. Making educated decisions about your money doesn't require being a financial wizard - it simply demands an open mind, a thirst for knowledge, and a willingness to adapt. It's this approach that can bring not just financial security but also peace of mind in your retirement. Remember, comfort in investing comes from understanding and managing your investments effectively. Happy investing!

# Chapter Nine

# Do you plan to work part-time after retirement?

R etirement is often considered the finish line - when you can kick back, relax, and savor the fruits of your labor. However, for many people, retirement is also a time for part-time work.

## Why Work Part-Time in Retirement?

For many retirees, the transition to retirement can be more of a gentle slide rather than a complete stop. But why opt for part-time work exactly? Here are a few reasons you might want to consider.

- **Financial Security**: Even with a well-planned retirement nest egg, an additional income source will help you manage finances better.

- **Stay Active**: Working part-time can help keep your mind sharp and active.

- **Social Interaction**: Workplaces allow interaction with others and building relationships.

In addition, here are some of the unique reasons beyond the usual suspects of financial security and staying active.

- **Reinvention**: Retirement can be an exciting opportunity to reinvent oneself. Part-time work can enable you to explore new fields or industries that you've always been interested in but never had the chance to delve into before. It's an adventure of discovery and learning, keeping life vibrant and exciting.

- **Legacy**: Some people choose to work to continue contributing to their field and building their legacy. Part-time work can help you maintain your professional identity and continue making a difference, albeit on a smaller scale.

- **Sense of Purpose**: Work often gives us a sense of purpose. Part-time work can help maintain that sense of purpose and create structure in our day-to-day lives. It can help bridge the gap between a full work schedule and the open-ended nature of retirement.

- **Mental Health**: Research shows that staying mentally active can help stave off cognitive decline. Part-time work, especially learning new skills or solving problems, can be a form of mental exercise.

The decision to work part-time post-retirement is very personal and can be influenced by various factors. Understanding all the potential benefits allows you to make an informed decision that best suits your retirement vision.

## Navigating the Part-Time Work Landscape

Entering the part-time work landscape post-retirement is not just about balancing work and leisure—it's about maneuvering a new territory that can be both rewarding and challenging. Here are some considerations to make when deciding to work part-time in retirement.

## Embrace Your Skills and Interests

Working part-time in retirement doesn't have to be an extension of your previous career. It's an opportunity to combine your accumulated skills with your interests and passions. Perhaps you've retired from a corporate job yet always had a soft spot for gardening. Now could be your chance to work part-time in a nursery or garden center or even start a small gardening advice blog.

## Balance Work and Leisure Time

Balancing work and leisure time is vital in making the most of your part-time work and retirement. While earning extra money can be a great bonus, ensure that work does not overshadow the relaxation and enjoyment aspects of your retirement. Consider a job that aligns with your hobbies or interests. This way, work won't feel like a chore but a fulfilling way to spend time.

## Tackle Challenges Head-On

Venturing into a new work landscape post-retirement can come with its unique challenges. You might face age bias, learn new skills, or adapt to a different work culture. Recognize these challenges and develop strategies to overcome them. Seek advice from others who have walked this path—you'll find their insights invaluable.

## Stay Open to Opportunities

Remain open to diverse opportunities. Perhaps a part-time job at a local bookstore, a consultancy gig based on your expertise, or even volunteering can lead to paid work. Diversifying your options can make the journey more fulfilling and less stressful.

## Next Steps: Prepping for the Part-Time Work

Once you've decided, it's time to prepare for this new chapter. Update your resume, harness your network, and prepare to enter the exciting world of part-time work in retirement. The next chapter awaits!

## Case Study: Part-Time Work in Retirement

Mrs. Patel recently retired after a 30-year career in academia. Instead of stepping entirely away, she decided to work part-time as a consultant for a non-profit organization. This provides her with additional income and the chance to use her skills meaningfully without the intense pressures of a full-time job.

Retirement doesn't have to mean the end of productive work. Many retirees find part-time work to be both financially rewarding and personally fulfilling. It can also be an excellent chance to pursue something you're passionate about. But remember, the choice to work part-time post-retirement is entirely personal, and what works for one person may not necessarily work for another. As you consider your next chapter, remember that retirement is about living the life you wish - whether that includes part-time work or not.

# Section 3 - Health Care Planning

Health becomes increasingly crucial as we age. This section provides suggestions for supplementing Medicare, estimating future health costs, and evaluating insurance to protect your assets. You'll also learn the importance of care directives and how to choose suitable options for your circumstances. With proper planning, you can feel empowered in managing your healthcare.

# Chapter Ten

# Considering the Medical Costs Associated with Aging

Approximately 10,000 Americans reach retirement age every day, a number set to remain constant for the next decade. One common question looming on the horizon of retirement planning is, "Have you considered the medical costs associated with aging?". This perspective is essential as healthcare will likely be one of the major expenses during retirement.

## The Truth about Healthcare Expenses for Pre-Retirees

Take a moment. Close your eyes and visualize your life post-retirement. You've bid farewell to the 9-to-5 grind, and now you can live your golden years as you've always dreamed. But amidst the tranquility, many overlook an uncomfortable reality – the looming healthcare expenses.

Truthfully, healthcare costs in the U.S. do not retire when you do. On the contrary, they continue to ascend. Based on a projection by HealthView Services, a healthy 65-year-old couple retiring this year might face around $662,156 in lifetime healthcare costs. This startling figure includes Medicare Parts B and D expenses and supplemental and dental insurance.

So, if you're planning for retirement, these numbers aren't just statistics. They outline the healthcare financial landscape you might need to navigate in your later years. This realization can feel daunting, but securing a stress-free retirement is crucial. The key lies in understanding the factors contributing to these escalating costs and finding workable strategies to manage them efficiently.

## Unraveling the Hidden Triggers Behind Soaring Healthcare Costs

The mounting medical costs in your golden years are not a result of random chance but the consequence of several interlocked factors. You might already know some culprits, like inflation in medical services, health insurance, prescription drugs, and an increase in chronic conditions and longer life expectancy. But let's unravel a few less-discussed triggers that are silently inflating your healthcare bill:

- **Rise of Specialty Drugs**: The pharmaceutical industry continuously advances, bringing new treatments for previously untreatable conditions. However, these specialty drugs come with a hefty price tag, contributing significantly to the upward trend of healthcare costs.

- **Administrative Costs**: The U.S. healthcare system is known for its complex administration, a factor that often gets overlooked. A fraction of every healthcare dollar is spent on administration, increasing overall costs.

- **Aging Population**: As the U.S. population profile ages, the increased demand for care services may lead to higher prices. The elderly often need more intensive and expensive healthcare, which can drive up costs for everyone.

While these factors may seem intimidating, understanding them better equips you to tackle the financial challenges that accompany aging. Let's look at some practical strategies to combat these escalating costs.

## Ways to manage healthcare costs as you age

Healthcare planning should be integral to your retirement planning to ensure escalating healthcare costs don't tarnish your golden years. Some suggestions to this end:

- Maximizing your Medicare: Utilize all the preventive services and screenings covered by Medicare.

- Long-term Care Insurance: Consider purchasing long-term care insurance, which covers health care services and support for your daily activities.

- Health Savings Account (HSA): Contribute towards an HSA as they provide a triple tax benefit.

## Innovative Approaches to Manage Healthcare Costs as You Age

Proper healthcare planning should be integral to your retirement plan to ensure escalating healthcare costs don't tarnish your golden years.

While important, traditional advice like maximizing your Medicare benefits, considering long-term care insurance, and contributing to an HSA are not the only ways to safeguard your health and wealth. Here are some lesser-known strategies to consider:

- **Telehealth Services**: As technology advances, telehealth becomes an increasingly viable option. Offering convenience and lower costs, virtual consultations can help manage your healthcare costs without compromising the quality of care.

- **Preventive Care & Wellness Programs**: Many insurance companies offer incentives for members who engage in preventative health and wellness activities. These programs can save money and help prevent or manage chronic conditions.

- **Medical Cost-Sharing Programs**: These programs involve individuals sharing healthcare costs, providing an alternative to traditional health insurance. They often result in lower payments but may not cover all healthcare costs.

- **Negotiate Medical Bills**: Many people don't realize that medical bills can often be negotiated down or payment plans can be arranged. Directly discussing your bills with your healthcare provider could lead to potential savings.

Remember, when planning for retirement, it's crucial to consider the inevitable health costs you will face with aging. By thinking out of the box and utilizing these strategies, you can manage these costs effectively and enjoy a comfortable, fulfilling retirement.

As you plan for retirement, it's crucial to understand and consider the inevitable health costs you will face with aging. With proper planning, education, and utilizing the resources available, you'll be

well-equipped to manage these costs and enjoy a comfortable, fulfilling retirement. Having a comprehensive, clear-cut plan will help
you reduce the stress associated with the financial aspects of aging,
leaving you more time and energy to focus on enjoying those golden
years. Be proactive about outlining and implementing your healthcare
plan to keep your retirement savings intact and extend their timeline.
Remember, planning can simplify your retirement years.

# Chapter Eleven

## Are You Fully Covered?

Whether you're a young professional starting to think about retirement or a seasoned veteran nearing that actual day, one of the pressing questions you need to answer is: How fully covered are you with insurance?

### Understanding the Importance of Insurance in Retirement

For many individuals preparing for retirement, the focus often lies on savings, investments, and pensions. While these aspects are undeniably crucial, the importance of having comprehensive insurance coverage should never be underestimated.

### Health Insurance

Primarily, health becomes a top concern as one ages. Individuals over 50 are more likely to face health issues; health-related costs can significantly affect your retirement savings. Consequently, ensuring that your health insurance plan provides adequate coverage is essential.

- Verify the extent of your health insurance coverage

- Check if it incorporates long-term healthcare provisions

- Evaluate if it offsets the increased health risks associated with aging

## Life Insurance

Life insurance can provide a reliable safety net despite being less crucial than health insurance. This especially applies to those with dependents or outstanding debts.

- Determine the need for life insurance based on your family's financial needs.

- Analyze whether the policy's maturity will coincide with your retirement

## Home and Auto Insurance

Generally, the need for home and auto insurance may remain constant even after retirement. However, there may be opportunities for cost savings.

- Evaluate the possibility of trimming your home or auto insurance

- Look into discounts offered for retirees

## How Your Insurance Needs Change As You Age

As we enter different stages of life, our insurance needs inevitably shift. Understanding these changes is crucial to ensure we have the right coverage during our retirement years.

## Health Insurance Adjustments

As you age, your health insurance needs will increase. You may need more comprehensive coverage for routine check-ups, prescription medications, and chronic disease management. If you haven't already, consider plans that cover long-term care, as the need for assisted living or nursing home care can arise as you age.

## Life Insurance Modifications

In your early years, life insurance might have been crucial for protecting your dependents in case of your untimely demise. As you age and your children become independent, your focus might shift from income replacement to using life insurance as a tool for estate planning or leaving a legacy.

## Home Insurance Changes

Your home insurance needs may alter based on where you decide to live during your retirement years. If you choose to downsize, you may need less coverage. Conversely, if you move to an area prone to natural disasters, you may need to contemplate additional coverage.

## Auto Insurance Alterations

As you age, the frequency of your driving may reduce, which might lower your auto insurance premium. However, statistical risks associated with older drivers (like slower reflexes and poorer eyesight) might cause your rates to increase. Discussing these changes with your insurance provider to ensure you're not overpaying while maintaining adequate coverage is essential.

Remember, reassessing your insurance needs as you age is as important as the initial purchase. Regular reassessment ensures that your coverage evolves with your changing lifestyle, providing peace of mind in your golden years.

## The Metrics for Assessing Insurance Coverage

Assessing the adequacy of your insurance coverage involves more than a mere glance at your policy documents. Here's a detailed step-by-step guide to help you gauge your current coverage:

1. **Review Your Policies in Detail:** Start by taking a comprehensive look at your current insurance policies. Understand the terms, exclusions, limits, and deductibles for each policy. Note down any terms or areas you find confusing.

2. **Create an Inventory of Your Needs:** Next, consider your lifestyle, health status, family responsibilities, and financial obligations. What kind of coverage do you need now and anticipate needing in the future? Is your current coverage adequate, or are there gaps or redundancies?

3. **Consult an Insurance Expert:** Insurance jargon can be complex, and understanding policy terms can be challenging. An insurance expert or a financial advisor can simplify this process. They can answer your questions and guide you

in better understanding your coverage and identifying potential gaps.

4. **Compare with Similar Policies:** Understand how your current coverage compares to other policies in the market. Are you getting the best deal, or are there better options available?

5. **Plan for Regular Reviews:** Insurance is not a one-time affair. Ensure you review your coverage periodically or whenever there's a significant change in your life, such as a health issue, a new dependent, or a change in your financial obligations.

This comprehensive approach will help protect you and your loved ones during retirement. Remember, insurance isn't just about protection but peace of mind.

Retirement should be a time of relaxation, ease, and enjoyment. But without proper planning, it can become a period filled with worries and financial struggles. Assessing your insurance coverage is an essential piece of the retirement puzzle. It is crucial to remember that insurance needs change as we age, and so our plans must be reviewed and updated periodically.

Are you fully covered with insurance? If you are unsure, now is the time to reassess. It's never too early to ensure that you and your loved ones are adequately protected.

# Chapter Twelve

# What Are Your Options for Purchasing Supplemental Health Insurance?

A s we edge closer to the golden years of retirement, our health inevitably becomes a priority. The costs related to healthcare can quite quickly add up, making supplemental health insurance a beneficial investment. We aim to help you understand your options regarding supplemental health insurance.

## Understanding Supplemental Health Insurance

Supplemental health insurance is an additional plan designed to cover costs that your primary health insurance does not cater to. These costs can include copayments, deductibles, coinsurance, and services not covered by your primary health insurance.

This type of insurance can be a significant safety net since health-care costs can escalate quickly due to unexpected illnesses or accidents. Without it, you may be burdened with medical bills that your primary insurance won't cover, potentially leading to financial hardship.

Many believe their primary health insurance will absorb all their health expenses. However, this often isn't the case, as many insurance plans have gaps in coverage. That's where supplemental health insurance fills these coverage gaps and provides a broader safety net. This insurance type can prove particularly beneficial for those with a high risk of certain diseases due to genetics or lifestyle factors, those who participate in risky activities, or those who want the peace of mind that comes with comprehensive coverage.

Remember that while supplemental health insurance can provide valuable additional coverage, it's not intended to be used as a stand-alone plan. Instead, it's meant to complement your primary health insurance, further cushioning you financially against the high healthcare costs.

## Options for Purchasing Supplemental Health Insurance

Supplemental health insurance has options designed to address specific healthcare and financial needs. You are not limited to one or two choices. Here are several viable options for you to consider:

- **Medigap**: This insurance plan, purchasable from a private company, covers costs such as copayments, coinsurance, and yearly deductibles not covered by Medicare. It's ideal for those anticipating regular hospital visits or specialist treatment but usually doesn't cover services like vision and dental care.

- **Medicare Advantage**: An alternative to Medicare, this plan can cover additional benefits such as vision, dental, and even some prescriptions. It's a comprehensive plan with more extensive coverage than basic Medicare, but it might incur higher out-of-pocket costs.

- **Critical Illness Insurance**: This insurance pays out a lump sum if you get diagnosed with one of the specific illnesses it covers. It is a good choice if you have a family history of certain diseases, but remember, it only covers specified illnesses.

- **Hospital Indemnity Insurance**: This plan covers costs related to hospital stays that are not typically covered by traditional health insurance. It can be beneficial if you want to cover unplanned hospitalization costs but bear in mind that it doesn't cover outpatient treatment.

- **Accident Health Insurance**: This insurance covers costs relating to any accidents, helping you with the deductibles and copays usually left by primary health insurance. It's ideal for those who engage in high-risk activities, but remember, it only engages when an accident occurs.

Remember, each insurance type has pros and cons; understanding these is essential before deciding. Consulting with a trustworthy insurance agent can be worthwhile to help you navigate these options.

## Some Valuable Tips

Navigating the world of supplemental health insurance requires careful consideration and informed decision-making. Here are some tips to guide you through this process:

1. **Understand Your Primary Health Insurance**: Conduct a

thorough review of your primary health insurance to understand precisely what it covers and where the gaps lie. Many assume their basic insurance covers more than it does, leading to unforeseen expenses and financial strain.

2. **Evaluate the Costs**: It's not just about the cost of the supplemental plan but also the out-of-pocket costs you'd incur without it. Factors in potential scenarios include hospital stays, specialist treatments, and even long-term care, which can quickly add up.

3. **Get Expert Advice**: Guidance from a trustworthy insurance agent can be invaluable in navigating the myriad of options available. They can help you understand the terms and conditions associated with each plan and provide insight into insurance providers' reputation and reliability.

4. **Consider Unexpected Scenarios**: It's easy to dismiss certain insurance types if you lead a low-risk lifestyle. However, remember that health is unpredictable, and your needs may change.

5. **Debunk Misconceptions**: Remember, supplemental health insurance is designed to complement, not replace, your primary health insurance. It's also not a one-size-fits-all solution. Your needs may differ significantly from others, so choosing a plan that fits your individual health and financial circumstances is essential.

With these tips in mind, you'll be better equipped to make an informed decision about supplemental health insurance. This can provide you with valuable peace of mind, knowing that you're prepared for whatever health-related expenses come your way.

With various options available, purchasing supplemental health insurance can be beneficial to protect your finances and health in your golden years. However, it's essential to take your time, research, and preferably get professional advice when considering which supplemental health insurance is the most appropriate for your needs. Remember, health is your greatest wealth, especially when retiring!

# Last Will and Testament

## of

_____

_____, resident in the City of _____, being of sound
_____ or undue influence, and fully understanding the nature
_____ and of this disposition thereof, do hereby make, publish,
_____ my Last Will and Testament, and hereby revoke any
_____ etofore made by me.

_____ my last illness, funeral, and burial, be paid as
_____ convenient, and I hereby authorize my
_____ d, to settle and discharge, in his or her
_____ estate.

_____ pay out of my estate any and all
_____ death in respect of all items
_____ ing under this Will or otherwise
_____ if such taxes were my de
_____ ne who receives any

# Section 4 - Legal Planning

L egal preparation is essential for a stress-free retirement. Here, you'll learn the importance of estate planning and strategies to pass on your legacy securely. We discuss wills, trusts, powers of attorney, and other vital documents. With your legal affairs in order, you and your loved ones gain peace of mind.

# Chapter Thirteen

# Have You Updated Your Will Recently?

Preparing for retirement can be a complex process, with many essential tasks to accomplish and decisions to be made. Among these tasks, one that should not be overlooked is updating one's will.

If you are one of the 55+ individuals planning for retirement, it's crucial to ask yourself: have you updated your will recently? Let's explore why this is vital and what you should consider.

## The Importance of Updating Your Will

Your will is a living document that should reflect your current circumstances, including your assets, family structure, and retirement goals. Here's why keeping it updated is essential:

- **Reflecting Life Changes:** Your will should be revised following significant life events such as marriage, divorce, the birth of children or grandchildren, or the death of a loved one.

- **Asset Management:** Retirement often changes your assets, whether liquidating investments, acquiring new property, or selling assets. Ensure your will accurately reflects your financial landscape.

- **Executor and Beneficiaries:** Your chosen executor might no longer be the best fit due to changes in the relationship or their capacity to serve; likewise, you may wish to alter the beneficiaries of your estate.

- **Tax Implications:** Tax laws change frequently, and your will should be designed to minimize the tax burden on your estate, consistent with your wishes.

## Key Considerations When Updating Your Will

When revising your will, here are some key factors to bear in mind:

- **Legality and Compliance:** Ensure your updated will comply with current state laws to avoid legal issues for your heirs.

- **Inheritance Plans:** Clearly outline your inheritance wishes to avoid potential disputes and ensure your legacy is passed on as intended.

- **Trusts and Estates:** Explore if setting up trusts for your beneficiaries makes sense, mainly if you aim to protect assets or manage how your inheritance is distributed.

- **Guardianship:** For those with dependents, guardianship decisions are a critical component of a will. Ensure your wishes regarding the care of minors or dependents with special needs are up-to-date.

## When to Update Your Will

Timing can be as important as content when updating your will. Consider revisiting your will at these times:

- **Retirement Planning:** An updated will should be part of this process when making long-term retirement plans.

- **Annually:** An annual check to ensure your will still reflects your current situation is a good practice.

- **After Tax Changes:** Whenever there are substantial changes in tax laws that may affect your estate, it's time to review.

- **Life-Changing Events:** Anytime you experience significant life changes, your will should be updated accordingly.

Retirement marks a new chapter in life, and with it comes the need for peace of mind regarding your estate planning. Updating your will can ensure that your final wishes are honored and that your loved ones are cared for according to your wishes. Consider making it a routine part of your retirement planning to review and, if necessary, update your will with the assistance of a legal professional. Your future self and your family will thank you.

# Chapter Fourteen

# Who Will Make Decisions on Your Behalf If You Become Incapacitated?

As individuals approach retirement, one critical consideration often unaddressed is the question of incapacity. While most people plan financially for their retirement years, many overlook the importance of having a plan that outlines who will make decisions on their behalf should they become unable to do so. This is not just a matter for the elderly; unforeseen circumstances can incapacitate anyone. Below, we delve into the importance of this planning and what you should consider as you approach your golden years.

## Understanding Incapacity

Before diving into decision-making, it's essential to understand what incapacity means. Legally, incapacity refers to an individual's inability to manage their affairs due to physical or mental impairment. This can be a result of an accident, illness, or cognitive decline, such as dementia. Becoming incapacitated without an established directive can place a heavy burden on your loved ones and could lead to family disputes or even court intervention to manage your affairs.

## Planning Ahead

Preparing for incapacitation is a multi-step process. Here's what it typically involves:

## Choosing a Power of Attorney

- **Financial Decisions**: A financial power of attorney is a legal document granting someone you trust to handle your financial affairs. This can include paying bills, managing investments, and even selling property if necessary.

- **Health Care Decisions**: A health care power of attorney, sometimes called a health care proxy, allows a designated individual to make medical decisions on your behalf. This includes consenting to or refusing treatment, accessing your medical records, and deciding on living arrangements that best serve your health needs.

## Establishing a Living Will

- A living will is a document that outlines your wishes regarding medical treatment if you become terminally ill or permanently unconscious. This is especially important if your philosophy about end-of-life care differs from what your family might assume.

## Considering a Trust

- A revocable living trust can help manage your assets during your lifetime and offers a seamless transition if you become incapacitated. Unlike a will, it is effective immediately upon creation and enables the person you've chosen as trustee to step in without court intervention.

## Keeping Your Plan Up-To-Date

- Just as your life evolves, so too should your incapacity plan. Major life events such as marriage, the birth of a child, or the loss of a loved one can all necessitate a revision of your documents. Regularly reviewing and updating your documents ensures that they reflect your current wishes and circumstances.

## Communicating Your Wishes

Having these documents is crucial, but it's equally essential that the right people know they exist and understand your intentions.

- **Family Discussions**: It can be uncomfortable to discuss the possibility of becoming incapacitated, but open communication helps prevent misunderstandings and ensures your wishes are clear.

- **Legal and Financial Advisors**: Ensure that your attorneys and financial planners know who has power of attorney and where your documents are located.

- **Health Care Providers**: Discuss your wishes with your doctors and give them copies of your health care power of attorney and living will to include in your medical records.

In conclusion, planning for incapacitation is an integral part of retirement planning. By establishing clear directives, you are protecting your assets and your autonomy and sparing your loved ones the pain and confusion that can come from uncertainty and potential legal struggles. Remember, preparation is the key to peace of mind for you and those you care about. It's never too soon to start having these critical conversations and to put the necessary documentation in place.

# Chapter Fifteen

# Do You Need a Power of Attorney or a Health Care Directive?

C an you imagine waking up one day and finding your loved one has made decisions about your financial or personal affairs without fully understanding your wishes? Or worse, imagine being in a medical situation where you can't express your healthcare preferences, and your family is left in turmoil, uncertain of the right path to take. These scenarios are more common than you might think. Everyone, especially as we age or approach retirement, should contemplate the potential outcomes and take preemptive steps to maintain control over their life decisions. One crucial step in managing your affairs, even when you might not be physically or mentally capable, is considering whether you need a Power of Attorney or a Health Care Directive.

## Power of Attorney

A Power of Attorney (POA) is a legal document that permits you to designate someone to act on your behalf should you become unable to manage your property, finances, or medical affairs. To illustrate its importance, picture this: You're an avid traveler jet-setting globally. Unforeseen circumstances lead to you being stranded in a remote location with limited access to communications. Back home, your bills are piling up, your investments need critical decisions, and your property requires urgent maintenance. With a POA in place, you can rest assured that a trusted individual is taking care of your affairs according to your prior directions. Here are other reasons why you might need a POA:

- To prevent potential confusion and conflicts among family members who might have different opinions about managing your affairs

- To have a trusted confidante who can act in your best interests, ensuring your choices are respected and implemented

Remember, a POA is not just a document. Knowing that unexpected circumstances won't derail your life is a safeguard for your peace of mind.

## Health Care Directive

On the other hand, a Health Care Directive (HCD), also known as a living will or medical directive, gives someone the power to decide the health care they receive if they cannot communicate or make decisions. Let's consider a scenario. You're an adventurous individual who loves extreme sports. During one of your escapades, you suffer an accident and fall into a coma. With an HCD, you can ensure your healthcare preferences are known and followed even in such a situation. Here are a few more reasons for obtaining an HCD:

- Ensure that your health care wishes are fulfilled even if you become incapacitated. For instance, you might have strong feelings about being kept on life support or preferring palliative care.

- To protect your right to refuse medical treatment, you don't want or endorse the treatment you want, such as experimental therapies or alternative medical procedures.

- To reduce loved ones' stress about making medical decisions in a crisis, sparing them from the agony of second-guessing what they would have wanted.

By having an HCD, you can make your healthcare choices clear, guiding those who might need to make decisions on your behalf.

## So, Do You Need Them?

Whether or not you need a Power of Attorney or a Health Care Directive is a deeply personal decision and depends on various factors. These factors include your age, health condition, lifestyle, family dynamics, financial situation, and comfort level in delegating significant decisions to others.

To help you better determine if these documents are necessary for your specific situation, consider the following questions:

1. Do you often engage in high-risk activities or travels that could hinder you?

2. Do you have strong preferences about specific healthcare options or treatments?

3. Are you a primary decision-maker on significant financial matters, such as managing your investments or property?

If you answered 'yes' to any of these questions, you might want to consider setting up a Power of Attorney, a Health Care Directive, or both.

Remember, these documents are not about giving up control but ensuring that your wishes are followed when you cannot communicate them. As such, they can provide valuable protection and peace of mind. Consulting with a financial advisor or attorney can further clarify their necessity.

Life is an unpredictable journey filled with joyous adventures and unforeseen challenges. As we grow older, indulge in high-risk activities, or take on significant financial responsibilities, we must ensure our wishes are heard even when we can't voice them ourselves.

Documents like Power of Attorney and Health Care Directive are not mere pieces of paper. They embody your voice during times of uncertainty, a roadmap for your loved ones, and a testament to your wishes and preferences. They assure us that our lives can proceed as we want, even in our absence or incapacity.

Retirement is more than just a phase; it's a testament to years of hard work and experience. It's a time for relaxation, reflection, and enjoyment. Ensuring your affairs are well settled in advance is vital to enjoy this time without stress or worry truly. Investing now in steps like preparing a Power of Attorney or a Health Care Directive can provide you with the secure, serene, and self-assured retirement you've earned and deserve. After all, peace of mind is the best retirement gift you can give to yourself and your loved ones.

# Section 5 - Tax and Estate Planning

Taxes can take a massive bite out of retirement savings. This section explores techniques to minimize taxes on your income, investments, retirement accounts, and estate. You'll also learn how to gift assets and utilize trusts to reduce your taxable estate. Implementing savvy tax strategies can stretch your retirement dollars.

# Chapter Sixteen

# Tax Implications Of Your Retirement Accounts

R etirement accounts play a crucial role in fiscal planning for the retirement years. Not only do these accounts provide a source of income for your post-work years, but they can also have significant tax implications. Here, we examine the tax implications that various types of retirement accounts may hold for you.

### Traditional 401(k) or Traditional IRA

- Both the Traditional 401(k) and Traditional IRA offer the advantage of tax-deductible contributions. The money you contribute to these accounts gets deducted from your taxable income, potentially placing you in a lower tax bracket.

- However, the "catch" is that distributions from these accounts are taxed as ordinary income during retirement.

- As such, the tax benefits are "deferred," meaning you'll get taxed on the amount you withdraw in retirement rather than the amount you contribute in the present.

## Roth 401(k) or Roth IRA

- Unlike Traditional retirement accounts, contributions to Roth accounts do not offer a tax deduction.

- Instead, the benefits of Roth accounts come when you start to take distributions: they are tax-free during retirement as long as you meet certain conditions.

- Given this, if you anticipate being in a higher tax bracket during retirement, it may be advantageous to contribute to a Roth account now and pay the taxes upfront.

## 403(b) or 457(b) Plans

- These retirement accounts are available to employees of public schools and specific tax-exempt organizations.

- They work similarly to a Traditional 401(k); pre-tax contributions reduce your taxable income now but will be taxed upon distribution.

## Taxable Investment Accounts

- Taxable accounts do not offer the immediate benefits of the retirement accounts listed above but may offer more tax advantages in the long run.

- Unlike retirement accounts, there is no penalty for withdrawing money before a certain age.

- Moreover, profits might qualify for long-term capital gains rates, typically lower than income tax rates.

Understanding the tax implications of your retirement accounts is critical. It's also important to consider that these rules can change, so it's recommended to consult with a tax advisor or financial planner to ensure that you're maximizing your retirement savings and reducing your tax liability based on your circumstances. Remember that the information given is a general overview and may not apply directly to everyone's unique situation. Regularly review your situation and adapt your financial planning strategies accordingly.

# Chapter Seventeen

# Which Assets Should You Draw on First in Retirement?

Retirement is a stage that requires sound financial planning to ensure a comfortable post-employment life. Most individuals' questions regarding retirement finances are - "Which assets should you draw on first in retirement?" Below are some considerations that could help answer that question.

## Cash and Savings Accounts

Firstly, consider drawing from your cash savings or regular bank accounts. These assets are the most liquid, with little to no growth or interest earnings potential.

- Cash savings

- Regular checking accounts

These are good sources because they don't typically generate significant earnings compared to other investment options.

## Taxable Accounts

Once your cash resources deplete, considering utilizing your taxable accounts can be beneficial. These are holdings on which you have already paid taxes, typically consisting of holdings in brokerages and mutual funds:

- Individual or joint brokerage accounts

- Mutual funds

Proceeds from these accounts may be subject to capital gains tax, but drawing down these accounts can also lower your potential taxable estate.

## Tax-Deferred Accounts

After depleting the taxable accounts, consider using your tax-deferred retirement accounts. Making withdrawals from these accounts may incur taxes on any income and investment gains, but the money can grow tax-deferred until it's withdrawn.

- Traditional 401(k) or 403(b)

- Traditional Individual Retirement Accounts (IRA)

The importance of timing these drawdowns cannot be stressed enough to avoid heavy taxation.

## Roth Accounts

Lastly, you may want to tap into your Roth accounts, which offer tax-free withdrawals on both contributions and earnings, providing you meet specific conditions:

- Roth 401(k)

- Roth IRA

Roth accounts can be valuable as emergency reserves due to their tax-free distribution benefits.

The sequence given is a general order that might suit many retirees; however, individual financial situations greatly vary.

It's worth consulting with a certified financial advisor to review your retirement planning strategies regularly. An optimal withdrawal strategy could minimize the impact of taxes and extend the longevity of your retirement savings. Prioritizing spending down particular types of assets can make a significant difference in the lasting potential of your retirement funds.

Remember, retirement planning isn't a one-time event. It's a process. Tailoring a unique plan that considers your specific circumstances and adjusting that plan as market conditions and personal circumstances change will lead to the most successful retirement outcome.

# Chapter Eighteen

# How to Minimize Your Estate Taxes: Strategies for Future Retirees

As you approach retirement, estate planning becomes critical to ensuring your hard-earned assets are passed on to your loved ones most efficiently. With strategic planning, you can minimize the estate taxes that can otherwise take a significant bite out of your legacy. Below are several techniques to help individuals consider retirement to reduce their estate tax liabilities.

## Understand Estate Taxes

Estate taxes, often called the "death tax," are levied on the estate of a person who has passed away before the assets are transferred to the heirs. It's important to understand that these taxes can vary greatly depending on your state and the size of your estate.

## Federal Estate Tax

- The federal government imposes an estate tax, but it only affects estates exceeding a certain threshold, adjusted annually for inflation.

- In recent tax years, only several million-dollar estates are subject to federal estate tax.

## State Estate Tax

- Some states also have their own estate or inheritance taxes with varying thresholds and rates.

- Check with a tax professional to understand your state's specific regulations.

## Gifting Assets

### Annual Gift Tax Exclusion

- You can give away up to a certain amount per year to an individual without incurring gift tax.

- This reduces your estate's value while benefiting your heirs during your lifetime.

### Lifetime Gift Tax Exemption

- Apart from the annual exclusion, there's also a lifetime exemption amount.

- Consider utilizing this exemption as part of your estate planning strategy.

## Trusts and Estate Planning

### Irrevocable Trusts

- By placing assets in an irrevocable trust, you legally remove ownership, which can reduce your estate's size.

- Irrevocable life insurance trusts can exclude life insurance proceeds from your estate.

### Charitable Lead Trusts

- This type of trust allows you to donate to a charity of your choice for a set period, with the remainder going to your beneficiaries.

- It can provide significant estate and gift tax savings.

## Other Considerations

### Marital Transfers

- Be aware of unlimited marital transfer rules that allow you to leave assets to a spouse tax-free.

- Utilizing this can help defer estate tax until the second spouse passes.

## Business Succession Planning

- For those who own a business, a succession plan can help to minimize estate taxes and ensure a smooth transition.

By combining these strategies, individuals nearing retirement can effectively minimize the impact of estate taxes on their assets. Consulting with a seasoned financial planner or estate planning attorney who understands your unique situation will ensure you take full advantage of the tax-saving opportunities available while aligning with your retirement and legacy goals. It is never too early to start planning for the future to safeguard your wealth and your family's well-being.

# Section 6 - Decisions Related to Housing

Where to live is a significant decision when planning your retirement lifestyle. This section weighs options like downsizing, relocating, or aging in place. You'll learn how to modify your home for accessibility and safety as you age. With information on different housing models like retirement communities, you can choose what suits you best.

# Chapter Nineteen

# Considering Retirement: Home Sweet Home or New Horizons?

R etirement signifies a pivotal shift in lifestyle, which often entails making significant decisions about where to spend these golden years. Individuals on the cusp of this new chapter face the question: should they stay in their familiar nests or spread their wings and relocate? This weighty decision can impact financial security, social life, and overall well-being.

## The Comfort of Home

For many soon-to-be retirees, home is not just a physical space but a treasure trove of memories, a community hub, and a place of profound emotional attachment.

- **Emotional Attachment**: Leaving behind a place that has been a part of life's many milestones can be challenging. For some, the emotional bond with their home and neighborhood is a compelling reason to stay put.

- **Community Connections**: Established relationships and community ties play a pivotal role. Staying means maintaining these connections, networks that might have taken decades to build.

- **Familiarity and Routine**: The comfort of a known environment and the convenience of established routines can offer stability and security that is hard to replicate elsewhere. Familiarity with the area, from local shops to healthcare services, adds a layer of ease to daily life.

- **Cost-Effectiveness**: For some, staying in their current home can be more cost-effective, especially if the mortgage is paid off or housing costs are relatively low.

## Embracing Relocation

Conversely, some individuals view retirement as an opportunity to embrace change, whether for adventure, a better climate, or closer proximity to family.

- **Downsizing**: Relocating often involves downsizing, which can reduce living expenses and maintenance responsibilities while freeing up equity that can be used to bolster retirement funds.

- **Improved Quality of Life**: Moving to a location with a more agreeable climate or more decadent cultural offerings can significantly enhance quality of life. Retirement hotspots often cater to the needs and wants of retirees, providing a renewed sense of adventure and exploration.

- **Closer Family Proximity**: The desire to be closer to family, especially grandchildren, can be a solid motivator to relocate. It can rebuild family bonds and decrease the sense of isolation that may come with aging.

- **Access to Better Health Care**: A move can lead to improved access to specialized healthcare services and facilities, often a priority for those with health concerns.

## Deciding Factors

Making the ultimate decision on where to live in retirement isn't easy and typically involves weighing several factors:

- **Financial Considerations**: One's financial situation often dictates the feasibility of either option. Evaluating the cost of living in a new location versus the current one is critical.

- **Health and Mobility**: Personal health and mobility concerns can influence the choice. A home might need modifications for accessibility, or the need for specialized care could drive relocation.

- **Lifestyle Preferences**: Retirement can be the time to pursue long-held dreams. Whether it's a peaceful life in the countryside or the vibrant pulse of an urban setting, location influences the fulfillment of these aspirations.

- **Community Services**: The availability of senior-friendly community services can sway the decision. Some areas offer more vibrant senior communities with plentiful resources and activities.

## Making the Choice

Ultimately, the decision depends on individual priorities and circumstances. Both options present benefits and trade-offs, making it crucial for each individual to reflect on what they value most in retirement. For some, the comfort and security of their home are unparalleled, while others yearn for the thrill of a new environment and the promise of novel experiences. The perfect retirement setting is a personal choice shaped by a mosaic of financial reality, health considerations, and lifestyle dreams.

# Chapter Twenty

# Advantages and Disadvantages of Downsizing for Individuals Approaching Retirement

When considering retirement, one of the significant decisions that individuals in their 50s and beyond often face is whether to downsize their living arrangements. Downsizing refers to moving to a smaller home or apartment, which can be a crucial step for many as they approach this new chapter in life. Below, we will explore some of this decision's potential advantages and disadvantages.

## Advantages of Downsizing

Downsizing can offer myriad benefits for individuals considering retirement, including financial, practical, and emotional perks.

### Financial Benefits

- **Reduced Living Expenses:** Moving to a smaller home generally means lower utility bills, reduced maintenance costs, and possibly lower property taxes, which can significantly decrease monthly expenditures.

- **The Possibility of Mortgage-Free Living:** If you sell your current, larger home, the profits may cover the cost of a smaller place outright, potentially allowing you to live without a mortgage.

- **Cash Released for Retirement:** The equity unlocked from the sale of a larger home can boost your retirement savings, providing more funds for travel, hobbies, or unexpected health care costs.

## Practical Benefits

- **Less Maintenance and Upkeep:** A smaller home usually means less time, effort, and money spent on maintenance and routine tasks, allowing for more leisure time and less physical strain.

- **More Suitable Living Space:** Many choose to downsize to homes that are more accessible and easier to navigate, perhaps with fewer stairs, which can be beneficial as one's mobility decreases with age.

- **Easier to Leave for Extended Periods:** With fewer responsibilities at home, it becomes much easier to lock up and leave for vacations or prolonged visits with family and friends.

## Emotional Benefits

- **A Fresh Start:** Downsizing can mark the beginning of a new chapter, providing an opportunity to declutter, simplify one's lifestyle, and live more minimally.

- **Community Environment:** Smaller homes or retirement communities often bring like-minded individuals closer together, fostering social connections and a sense of belonging.

## Disadvantages of Downsizing

However, there are also specific challenges and downsides to downsizing that must be acknowledged.

## Emotional and Psychological Impact

- **Sentimental Loss:** Leaving a home full of memories can be emotionally challenging. The process of sorting through belongings can be taxing and sometimes means parting with cherished items due to space constraints.

- **Adjustment Period:** Adapting to a smaller space may feel restrictive initially, and some individuals may struggle to find new routines or a sense of home in a new environment.

## Financial and Practical Concerns

- **Cost of Moving:** Downsizing itself can be expensive when considering moving costs, real estate fees, and possible renovations needed in the new home to make it suitable.

- **Reduced Space for Family and Entertaining:** Smaller homes mean less room for hosting family gatherings or long-term guests, which can be a significant downside for those who enjoy these activities.

## Strategic Planning Required

- **Finding the Right Home:** Finding a smaller home that meets all your new needs may take significant time and effort, mainly if staying in the same community is a priority.

- **Consideration of Future Needs**: Ensuring the new home can accommodate future mobility or health-related issues is essential to avoiding further moves.

For those over 50, the decision to downsize as retirement approaches is significant. It entails carefully weighing financial savings and increased simplicity against the emotional hurdles and practical trade-offs. Each individual must closely examine their situation, preferences, and future goals to determine whether the advantages outweigh the disadvantages of their particular circumstances.

# Chapter Twenty-One

## Considering Retirement Options: Exploring the Benefits of Retirement Communities and Assisted Living

R etirement marks a significant transition in life where individuals often contemplate their living arrangements and the type of lifestyle they wish to lead during their golden years. For some, this may mean downsizing, moving closer to family, or relocating to a warmer climate. For others, moving into a retirement community or an assisted living facility becomes appealing, offering numerous advantages worth considering.

### The Appeal of Retirement Communities

Retirement communities are typically designed for adults 55 and older and cater specifically to the lifestyle of retirees. Here are some reasons why this could be an alluring option:

- **Maintenance-Free Living:**

Most retirement communities offer maintenance-free living, removing the burden of home repairs, lawn care, and snow removal. This enables retirees to spend more time pursuing hobbies, traveling, or enjoying a hassle-free life.

- **Built-In Social Network:**
Living among peers provides ample opportunities for social interaction, helping reduce feelings of loneliness and isolation. These communities often have an active and vibrant social calendar with events, clubs, and outings.

- **Safety and Security:**
These facilities often have security features, emergency response systems, and sometimes gated entrances, offering residents and their families peace of mind.

- **Amenities and Activities:**
Retirement communities commonly offer a variety of amenities, such as fitness centers, swimming pools, and dining facilities. They regularly schedule activities that promote health, well-being, and lifelong learning.

- **Downsizing without Compromise:**
Retirees can choose accommodations to fit their needs without the maintenance concerns of a larger home, often without giving up the comforts they're accustomed to.

- **Proximity to Healthcare:**
Many of these communities are close to medical facilities; some offer on-site health services, making healthcare more accessible.

## Advantages of Assisted Living Facilities

Assisted living facilities, while similar to retirement communities, offer a higher level of care and assistance. They can be an excellent choice for individuals needing help with daily activities. Here are some benefits:

- **Personal Care and Assistance:**
  They help with daily tasks such as bathing, dressing, and medication management, allowing residents to live more independently despite health challenges.

- **Customized Care Plans:**
  Care plans are tailored to each resident's unique needs, ensuring they receive the right assistance while maintaining as much independence as possible.

- **Nutritious Meals:**
  Assisted living facilities offer prepared meals that account for their residents' dietary needs and preferences, taking the worry out of meal planning and preparation.

- **Engaging Activities:**
  These facilities typically provide a variety of social and recreational activities that cater to different interests and abilities, helping to keep residents active and engaged.

- **Transportation Services:**
  For residents who no longer drive, transportation services can be a boon, helping them get to appointments, shopping, or other events outside the facility.

- **Round-the-Clock Staffing:**
  The availability of caregivers and staff members around the clock offers reassurance that help is always at hand should any emergencies arise.

As individuals consider retirement, weighing the benefits of various living arrangements, considering personal needs and preferences, and planning for a comfortable, secure, and fulfilling retirement life is crucial. Moving into a retirement community or an assisted living facility could be prudent for those who value convenience, community, and care. Touring prospective places, talking to current residents, and thoroughly understanding the services and costs involved is essential. With careful consideration, retirees can find a living situation that feels like home and supports their lifestyle and well-being during the years ahead.

# Chapter Twenty-Two

## Preparing Your Home for Aging-in-Place

Aging-in-place refers to the ability to live in one's own home and community safely, independently, and comfortably, regardless of age, income, or ability level. As you approach or enter retirement, it is crucial to consider adjustments to your home environment that support your evolving needs. These changes can preserve your independence, improve safety, and prevent accidents. Here are some considerations for modifying your home to age in place gracefully.

### Assessing Your Current and Future Needs

The first step in preparing your home for aging is to take stock of your current living situation. This involves a realistic assessment of mobility, health conditions, and the potential need for assistive devices in the future.

### Immediate Adjustments

- Lower shelf heights for easier access.

- Install brighter lighting to aid visibility, especially in hallways and stairways.

- Replace doorknobs with lever handles, which are easier to operate.

- Add non-slip mats in the bathroom to prevent falls.

## Long-Term Home Features

- Building a first-floor bedroom to avoid stairs.

- Consider a walk-in shower with a bench and hand-held shower heads.

- Widen doorways for potential wheelchair or walker access.

- Install a stairlift or a personal elevator if the budget allows.

## Safety Improvements

Creating a safe living environment is essential for aging-in-place. Here are some of the crucial areas that need attention:

## Falls Prevention

- Remove throw rugs or secure them with non-slip backing to prevent tripping.

- Clear paths of clutter that could cause falls.

- Install grab bars in crucial bathroom areas near the toilet and shower.

- Ensure that stairs are well-lit, have handrails on both sides and are clear of obstacles.

## Fire Safety and Emergency Preparedness

- Install smoke and carbon monoxide detectors on every floor.

- Keep fire extinguishers in accessible locations, especially in the kitchen.

- Plan for an emergency exit strategy and keep essential items like a flashlight and a mobile phone within reach.

## Technological Enhancements

Technology can be a powerful tool to aid seniors in living independently.

## Smart Home Devices

- Use voice-activated smart home systems to control lighting, heating, or locking doors.

- Install security cameras and motion sensors for enhanced safety.

- Consider medical alert systems that can notify emergency

services with a button.

## Communication

- Set up video call capability to contact family and healthcare providers.

- Use reminder systems for medication or appointments.

## Healthcare Accessibility

Managing health conditions is a crucial part of aging in place.

### Setting Up In-Home Care

- Arrange for delivery of medications and healthcare supplies.

- Identify space in the home for healthcare providers to visit or administer treatments.

### Mobility Around the House

- Look into mobility aids like walkers, scooters, or wheelchairs that might become necessary.

- Ensure these devices can navigate the home easily by planning for adequate space.

To sum up, preparing your home for aging-in-place involves a comprehensive look at your current lifestyle and anticipating changes that might come with aging. This preparation provides comfort and conserves your independence and ensures a safer living space, potentially extending the time you can spend in your beloved home. Seek the guidance of professionals in home design and healthcare to tailor these changes specifically to your needs and enjoy your golden years with peace of mind.

# Section 7 - Social Considerations

Retirement is not just about finances - maintaining social ties and community bonds is vital for fulfillment and mental sharpness. This section provides tips for keeping socially engaged through volunteering, lifelong learning, social gatherings, and reconnecting with old friends. Protecting your social network safeguards your quality of life.

# Chapter Twenty-Three

# The Importance of Social Networks in Retirement

R etirement is more than just a phase of life where one stops working. It's a period where significant changes occur in daily routines, social interactions, and lifestyle habits. One of the most critical aspects that can affect the quality of life during retirement is the presence of a robust social network.

## Understanding Social Networks in Retirement

Social networks refer to the groups of friends, family, colleagues, and acquaintances you regularly interact with. These networks are critical in providing emotional support, companionship, and practical help. Let's delve into why they are crucial for retirees.

- **Emotional Support**: Emotional well-being is paramount as one transition from a structured work life to the freedom of retirement. Friends and family offer a listening ear, a compassionate heart, and a supportive presence during this time.

- **Physical Health**: Studies show that those with a solid social circle have better physical health. Social interactions can encourage a more active lifestyle and promote positive health behaviors.

- **Mental Sharpness**: Regular interactions with various people can keep the mind agile and reduce the risks of mental decline that may come with age.

- **Purpose and Belonging**: Feeling needed and belonging helps retirees maintain a sense of purpose and identity, which is particularly important after leaving a lifelong career.

## Assessing Your Social Network

### Questions to Consider

It is essential to evaluate the strength of your social network. Here are some questions to ponder:

1. Who do you currently spend time with regularly?

2. How often do you engage in social activities?

3. Do you feel supported by those around you?

4. Can you count on friends or family for practical help if needed?

5. How much effort are you investing in maintaining or expanding your social network?

## Building a Social Network

If you find your network lacking, fear not; retirement can be an excellent time to build and expand your connections. Consider the following actions:

- **Join Local Clubs or Groups**: This is a fantastic way to meet people with similar interests, whether gardening, reading, or hiking.

- **Volunteer**: Volunteering offers dual benefits; it allows you to give back to the community while connecting with others.

- **Take Classes**: Learning something new, such as a language or a craft, can put you in touch with a diverse group of people.

- **Stay in Tech**: Social media and communication tools help keep in touch with distant friends and family members.

- **Reconnect**: Retirement is an opportunity to reconnect with old friends and make amends where needed.

A solid social network during retirement isn't just about staying busy; it's about maintaining your quality of life through connection, support, and engagement. If you're approaching retirement, now is the time to nurture your existing relationships and cultivate new ones. Remember, your social network is the key to a healthier retirement.

# Chapter Twenty-Four

---

# Maintaining and Improving Social Relationships Post-Retirement

R etirement marks a significant life transition, often involving changes to daily routines and social patterns. For those 50 and older, contemplating retirement, maintaining or even improving social relationships can significantly benefit overall well-being. Here are some strategies for keeping your social life active post-retirement.

## Strategies for an Active Social Life After Retirement

When you retire, your daily interaction with colleagues ends, which could lead to isolation if proactive steps are not taken. However, retirement also opens up many opportunities to engage with friends, family, and new acquaintances in ways that work schedules may have previously limited. Below are strategies to boost social engagement after you've stepped back from the workforce:

## 1. Volunteer Your Time

- Find causes you're passionate about and dedicate time to volunteering.

- Volunteering can introduce you to individuals with similar values and interests and enrich your life with purpose.

## 2. Join Clubs or Groups

- Look for clubs or interest groups that align with your hobbies, such as book clubs, gardening groups, or hiking clubs.

- This can be an excellent way to meet new people and stay physically and mentally active.

## 3. Enroll in Classes

- Take advantage of local community colleges' educational opportunities or join workshops catering to retirees.

- Participating in classes can help you learn new skills and interact with peers.

## 4. Get Involved in Community Events

- Attend local festivals, markets, or public events to socialize and enjoy entertainment.

- It's an easy way to stay connected with the community around you.

## 5. Travel and Meet New People

- Retirement can be the perfect time to travel, whether it's locally, nationally, or internationally.

- Travel can lead to meeting diverse groups of people and forming new friendships.

## 6. Use Technology to Stay Connected

- Embrace social media platforms to keep in touch with friends and family.

- Explore video calling software to maintain relationships with those who may not be geographically close.

## 7. Rekindle Old Friendships

- Reach out to friends with whom you've lost touch over the years.

- Retirement provides the time to reconnect and share life experiences.

## 8. Stay Physically Active Together

- Join a local gym or fitness class suitable for seniors where you can be social while staying healthy.

- Engaging in group sports or walking clubs can also promote social interaction.

## 9. Start a Regular Social Gathering

- Organize weekly or monthly catch-ups such as dinners, movie nights, or game evenings.

- Consistent gatherings can build strong social bonds.

## 10. Offer Your Expertise

- Use the skills and knowledge from your career to mentor others, consult, or teach.

- Sharing your expertise not only helps others but can also help you build relationships and feel valued.

## Final Thoughts

Retirement doesn't have to mean the end of a vibrant social life. On the contrary, it can serve as the beginning of a chapter filled with rich experiences and new friendships. Retirees can maintain and improve their social relationships by taking deliberate steps to reach out and connect with others. Whether through shared activities, lifelong learning, or embracing technology and travel, the potential for forging and deepening social ties is immense. Enjoy this new phase of life as a time to engage with others and share the wealth of knowledge, stories, and time that retirement affords.

# Chapter Twenty-Five

---

# Have You Considered Volunteering or Mentoring in Retirement?

A s we approach the golden years of retirement, a horizon free from the daily grind beckons, promising rest, relaxation, and the pursuit of long-neglected hobbies. However, for many, retirement isn't solely about stepping back from a lifetime of work; it's about stepping into new roles that enrich their lives and those of others. Volunteering and mentoring are two pathways that can offer a sense of purpose, fulfillment, and connection in retirement.

## The Benefits of Volunteering and Mentoring

For those pondering retirement, here's why you might want to consider volunteering or mentoring as part of your next chapter:

## Personal Growth and Lifelong Learning

- Engaging in volunteer work can be a potent catalyst for personal growth. It often requires you to adopt new skills or sharpen existing ones, keeping your mind engaged and active.

- As a mentor, you become both a teacher and a student. The experience can offer a fresh perspective on life and introduce you to new ideas and cultures.

## Social Connection and Sense of Community

- Volunteering brings you into contact with people from diverse walks of life, fostering new friendships and strengthening community bonds.

- Mentoring can create lasting connections with individuals who greatly benefit from your wisdom and attention.

## Health and Well-being Benefits

- Studies have suggested that volunteering can positively affect mental health, including reductions in stress and depression.

- Being a mentor can instill a sense of purpose and belonging, which has been linked to overall well-being and even longevity.

## Giving Back and Making a Difference

- Retirement is an opportunity to give back to the community supporting you throughout your working years.

- As a volunteer or mentor, you have the unique privilege of making a tangible difference in the lives of individuals and organizations.

## Potential Volunteering Opportunities

When considering where to volunteer, the options are nearly limitless. Here are just a few to explore:

- **Local Community Centers**: They often need assistance with various programs and events.

- **Youth Organizations**: Share your expertise by mentoring the younger generation.

- **Non-Profit Organizations**: Help with fundraising, administration, or outreach.

- **Healthcare Facilities**: Provide support to staff, patients, and families.

## Stepping into a Mentorship Role

As a mentor, you have an array of options on how to engage with mentees:

- **Professional Mentorship**: Guide those still in or entering the workforce in your area of expertise.

- **Academic Tutoring**: Support students in subjects you are knowledgeable about.

- **Life Skills Coaching**: Help individuals navigate the complexities of everyday life.

## How to Get Started

If you are considering volunteering or mentoring, start by:

- Reflect on your interests and skills to find a suitable match.

- Research organizations in your community that can use your help.

- Reach out to volunteer coordinators to discover available opportunities.

- Network with fellow retirees who are already volunteering or mentoring.

Retirement opens a fresh chapter not just for leisure but for legacy. Through volunteering and mentoring, you can continue to grow, connect, and contribute in retirement, turning a period of culmination into one of commencement.

# One Last Thing...

If you enjoyed this book or found it useful I'd be very grateful if you'd post a short review on Amazon. Your support makes a difference, and I read all the reviews personally to get your feedback and make this book even better.

Thanks again for your support!

# About The Author

**L**ee Hathaway is an indie-published Amazon author. He lives in Elkhorn, Nebraska, with his wife and two children. Lee loves learning and inspiring others and has become a bit obsessed with thinking about retirement.

# Disclaimer Notice

B y reading this book, you acknowledge and agree that neither the author nor the publisher has any obligation, liability, or responsibility for any loss, injury, or damages, whether financial, personal, or otherwise, resulting from the direct, indirect, or proper use of this book's content or its application. The information provided is to the best of their knowledge and based on the author's experiences and research. However, readers are advised to consult with their legal, financial, or other professional advisors as deemed necessary before utilizing any advice or applying any techniques mentioned in this book.

The user of this book further understands that individual results may vary and that the success achieved by applying the ideas and strategies presented herein depends on the reader's circumstances, diligence, and personal efforts. The author and publisher cannot guarantee that the reader will experience any specific outcome or attain a specific goal by using this book's content.

Additionally, any opinions or views expressed in this book are of the author alone and do not reflect the opinions or views of the publisher or any associated entities. While every attempt has been made to ensure the accuracy and reliability of the information provided, errors and omissions may occur. The author and publisher expressly disclaim responsibility for any discrepancies or inaccuracies found within this book.

www.ingramcontent.com/pod-product-compliance
Lightning Source LLC
Chambersburg PA
CBHW020525290526
45786CB00002B/759